MINI PATCHWORK PROJECTS

6 Sewing Patterns for the Contemporary Crafter

BETH STUDLEY

David and Charles

www.stitchcraftcreate.co.uk

CONTENTS

A LITTLE OF WHAT YOU FANCY ...

Sometimes I find I am in the mood to sew but don't want to work on a big project. It's great, every now and then, to start and finish a project before you even need a break. Mini projects such as the ones in this book are perfect as handmade gifts and all useful sewing accessories that you can just make for yourself. There is somewhere to keep your pins, and your needles, somewhere to hang up all your inspiration, a place to keep your notes and designs, storage for your bits and bobs and even somewhere to put your cup down.

The fabrics used are designed by me and are from my fourth collection for Makower, which is called Radiance. This is a collection that took its inspiration from antique lace and trimmings. You will be able to buy it in shops or online if you would like to use the same ones or there are a variety of pre-cut fabric sizes that would be ideal for many of the projects.

Each project uses patchwork or quilting or both, and ranges in difficulty from beginner to advanced. There is a variety of techniques used throughout the projects, from basic patchwork, paper piecing, quilting, sewing darts, making binding and hand sewing. Each is in small doses so nothing will be too much to take on – just get on and enjoy yourself!

MATERIALS

THE BASIC THREE

The main components of all quilting projects are your fabric, wadding and thread.

Fabric – all the following projects use quilting weight cotton. This is generally available in a width of 44in (115cm). Mini projects such as these, that don't require large quantities, are fantastic for using 'pre-cuts'. These are a way of buying fabric in smaller quantities that are pre-cut into shapes that are useful for quilting. For example strips or squares. Where relevant, projects in this book will state when standard pre-cuts, such as charm packs (5in squares) or 'Layer Cakes' (10in squares), could be used.

Wadding (batting) – natural fibre waddings are best. Select 100% cotton or a cotton-bamboo mix.

Thread – use 100% cotton and select a good quality thread. This is particularly important for quilting where the stitches are visible and decorative.

EXTRAS

Self-cover buttons – these come in a variety of sizes and the back can vary between brands. They will always require you to cut a circle of fabric to cover a slightly curved base. Follow the instructions provided with the particular brand you have.

Standard buttons – the choices here are endless so it is up to you which style you choose for your project. Pick one that compliments the fabric you are using and does not over-power it.

Magnets – the size used in the Picture Garland project is ¾in (2cm). You could use different sized or shaped magnets but you may need to adjust the width of the holders accordingly.

Embroidery thread – I use 100% cotton thread in my work. There are many brands of embroidery thread these days that vary in price and are available in hundreds of colours.

Felt – I have used a lightweight acrylic felt as I happened to have some of this in my craft room! It comes in a wide variety of colours. Wool felt is slightly heavier and more natural looking and also looks great.

SEWING KIT

Pins – you will need to use pins for most of the projects in this book. I really recommend you invest in some good quality ones. Often cheap pins are not completely smooth. Even the slightest irregularity can cause a snag in the fabric or just simply make it hard to insert. Specialist quilting pins tend to be longer, sharper and smooth. Choose glass headed ones as they will not melt if you go over them with the iron.

Scissors – you will need both fabric and paper scissors.

Rotary cutting equipment – rotary cutter, self-healing mat and ruler. Rotary cutting is a quick and accurate way of cutting fabric. It is the most common way of cutting strips and shapes in quilting. It allows you to cut more than one layer of fabric at a time with ease, and also to cut a variety of shapes and angles easily. There are many tutorials to be found online if you would like more instruction on how to do this.

Iron – You don't need a special iron but do always make sure it's clean if you are going to use it for your sewing projects. I always use steam to help press things neatly.

Sewing machine – all the projects are written assuming a sewing machine will be used. If you are sewing by hand some aspects of the projects will need to be adapted.

Seam ripper – this is helpful if you make a mistake and need to unpick a seam. But it can also be a useful tool to cut threads.

Turning tool – you will need a blunt pointed tool like a knitting needle or BBQ skewer to help you when turning things right side out.

PICTURE GARLAND

· ·

Here's a neat little trick for displaying some of your favourite images so that you can have them festooning your creative corner, to inspire you or just cheer you up. It's a great way to keep notes or fabric samples in reach too, and it's really easy to make. You will wonder why you hadn't thought of it already!

· ·

Experience level: beginner

Techniques needed: rotary cutting

YOU WILL NEED

- Fabric 1, 3 x 6in (7.5 x 15cm)
- Fabric 2, 3 x 6in (7.5 x 15cm)
- Fabric 3, 3 x 6in (7.5 x 15cm)
- Fabric 4, 3 x 6in (7.5 x 15cm)
- Fabric 5, 3 x 6in (7.5 x 15cm)
- Fabric 6, 3 x 6in (7.5 x 15cm)
- Fabric 7, 3 x 6in (7.5 x 15cm)
- Fabric 8, 27 x 4in (69 x 10cm)
- 14 magnets, 2cm (¾in) You could use different size or shape magnets but you may need to adjust the width of the holders accordingly.
- Co-ordinating thread
- Sewing kit (see Materials)
- Turning tool (such as a knitting needle)

NOTES

All seam allowances are ¼in (5mm) unless otherwise stated.

WS = wrong side(s)

RS = right side(s)

MAKE THE MAGNETIC HOLDERS

1. Cut each of the 3 x 6in (7.5 x 15cm) pieces into four pieces measuring 3 x 1½in. Separate them into pairs and place RS together, lining up the edges. You will have 14 pairs.

2. Sew each pair together around three sides to create a pocket (see fig 1).

3. Trim the seams back to ⅛in (3mm) and turn RS out. Use a blunt pointy tool like a knitting needle to push right into the corners and press well. When all pieces have been sewn, insert a magnet into each pocket.

4. Pair them up, allowing the magnets to stick together, so you now have seven sets. Neaten them up so the edges match and trim any excess threads from the openings.

MAKE THE BINDING STRIP

1. Cut the fabric 8 piece in half to get two pieces measuring 2 x 27in (5 x 69cm). Sew together end to end to create a strip about 54in (138cm) long. Press the joining seam open.

2. Place RS down and fold over both of the long edges ¼in (5mm) to the WS. Press well. (See fig 2).

3. Fold the strip in half along the whole length, carefully lining up the folded edges. Press well to get a defined crease.

ADD THE MAGNETIC HOLDERS

1. Find the centre of the binding strip by folding it in half, short end to short end. Mark the centre with a pin. Lay the strip on a flat surface with the folded edges facing up.

2. Take the first of the magnet sets and place it, in the centre, where you marked with a pin. Make sure the raw edges touch the centre fold. Fold the strip back in half again sandwiching the magnetic holder inside, then pin in place. Place the rest of the magnet sets either side of the first at a spacing of 5in (12.5cm) as shown in figure 3.

4. Sew together ⅛in (3mm) from the folded edges of the strip, securing the magnetic holders in place.

MAKE THE HANGING LOOPS

1. Fold over each short end of the binding strip by ¼in (5mm) and press. Fold over again, this time by 1in (2.5cm), and press again.

2. Stitch in place close to the first fold to create a loop.

Figure 1

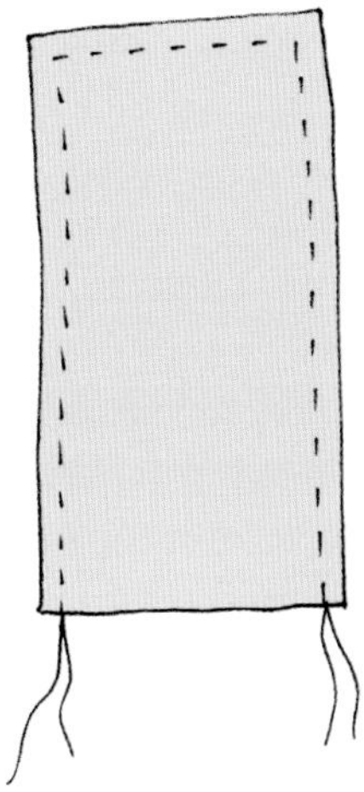

Figure 2

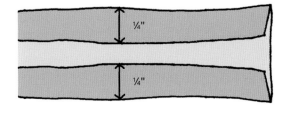

Figure 3

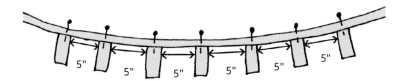

REVERSIBLE TRINKET BOWLS

....

Not only are these pretty fabric baskets perfect
for keeping all your threads and trinkets from
taking over the place, they are also reversible.
Whenever you feel like a change, just give them
a satisfying little flip to pop them inside out.

....

Experience level: medium

Techniques needed: using templates,
sewing darts, quilting

YOU WILL NEED

- Fabric 1, 10 x 10in (25 x 25cm)

- Fabric 2, 10 x 10in (25 x 25cm)

  You could use a 10in (25cm) charm pack/Layer Cake pre-cut for the fabrics in this project

- Cotton wadding (batting), 10 x 20in (25 x 50cm)

- Co-ordinating thread

- Sewing kit (see Materials)

- Pen (fabric or ballpoint)

NOTES

All seam allowances are ¼in (5mm) unless otherwise stated.

WS = wrong side(s)

RS = right side(s)

RST = right sides together

WSO = wrong side out

RSO = right side out

A walking foot is recommended throughout

Templates can be found at the end of this book

PREPARATION

Cut the wadding (batting) into two 10in (25cm) squares, then print and cut out the paper template. There are eight darts marked on the template. These will be cut out of the template at a later stage but for now, leave them just as they are.

PREPARING THE SIDES OF THE BOWL

1. Take the square of fabric 1 and place it, RS up, on top of one of the wadding squares. Line up the raw edges and pin around the edges to secure in place.

2. Starting in one corner, quilt in a wavy line, diagonally to the opposite corner. Continue to quilt diagonal lines approximately ½in (1cm) apart either side until the whole square is covered. Repeat on the opposite diagonal so that you create a grid (see fig 1).

3. Place the template, centrally, on top of the RS of the square and draw around it. You could use a fabric pen, but just a normal ballpoint pen would be fine.

4. Cut it out and repeat these stages for fabric 2 and the other wadding square.

SHAPING WITH DARTS

1. Take the template and cut the marked darts out of it, then take the first bowl side and place the template on the WS lining up the edges.

2. Mark the darts with the pen by drawing round the shape of the eight triangles you cut out. Starting at the first dart, fold the fabric RST, through the centre of the marked lines (see fig 2).

3. Starting at the wide end of the dart, sew following the marked line. Sew all the way to the point and off the end of the fabric. Then trim the excess fabric of the dart back to ⅛in (3mm). See fig 3.

4. Sew all the darts in this way and repeat for the second side of the bowl.

Figure 1

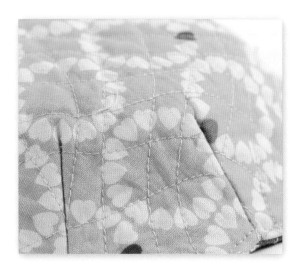

Figure 2

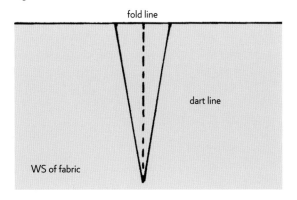

fold line

dart line

WS of fabric

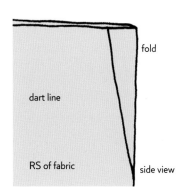

fold

dart line

RS of fabric

side view

Figure 3

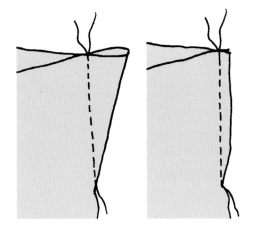

SEW THE TWO SIDES TOGETHER

5. Once both pieces have been shaped, turn one of them so the RS of the fabric is on inside. Now place the other one inside so you have one inside the other with RS together. Pin in place around the top. Ensure that you line up the raw edges and darts exactly. Sew together around the top leaving a turning gap between two of the darts (see fig 4).

6. Trim the seams back to ⅛in (3mm) all round apart from at the turning gap. Turn RS out and finger press the top of the bowl all the way round to manipulate it into shape. Then press with an iron.

7. Carefully turn the seams inside at the turning gap. Pin in place and press well. Stitch a line all around the top of the bowl ⅛in (3mm) from the edge, closing the turning gap in the process.

....

T I P S

It can be tricky to neatly turn in the seams at turning gap, particularly on a curve such as this. To make this easier, after pressing the bowl, use a seam ripper to make a second turning gap in one of the other curves. Turn the bowl back WSO and close the original turning gap. Trim the seam back to ⅛in (3mm) and then turn RSO again through the new gap. Because this gap has already had its seams pressed into a neat curve you will find it easier to turn them inside and pin neatly.

If you want to use the template again simple draw a straight line between the curved sections where you cut out the darts.

....

Figure 4

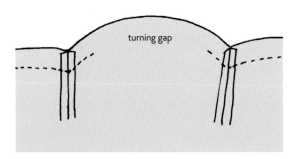

turning gap

PETALLED PIN CUSHION

Pretty and practical – the two essential requirements for the perfect pin cushion. The petals are simply made by pulling the fabric inwards with embroidery thread to create the flowery shape. Use pre-cut charm squares, or just scraps of your favourite fabrics.

Experience level: medium

Techniques used: using templates, hand sewing, sewing a Y-seam/inset seam

YOU WILL NEED

- Fabric 1 for the pin cushion top, 5 x 4in (12.5 x 10cm)

- Fabric 2 for the pin cushion top, 5 x 4in (12.5 x 10cm)

- Fabric 3 for the pin cushion top, 5 x 4in (12.5 x 10cm)

- Fabric 4 for the pin cushion top, 5 x 4in (12.5 x 10cm)

- Fabric 5 for the pin cushion top, 5 x 4in (12.5 x 10cm)

    You could use a 5in (12.5cm) charm pack pre-cut for fabrics 1 to 5 in this project

- Fabric 6, one 8in (20cm) square and two 2in (5cm) squares

- Co-ordinating thread

- Sewing kit (see Materials)

- Hand sewing needle

- Polyester toy stuffing, you can buy this in a standard 9oz (250g) bag. You will need four or five handfuls for this pin cushion

- 1yd (1m) co-ordinating embroidery thread

- Two ½in (1cm) self-cover buttons

NOTES

All seam allowances are ¼in (5mm) unless otherwise stated.

WS = wrong side(s)

RS = right side(s)

Templates can be found at the end of this book

PIECING THE TOP

1. Use the top template to cut pieces from each of the fabrics 1 to 5.

2. Starting with fabrics 1 and 2, place them RS together lining up the edges and sew down one edge as shown in figure 1.

3. Press the seam open, then take fabric 3 and sew to the edge of fabric 2 and again, press the seam open (see fig 2).

4. Take fabrics 4 and 5 and sew them together and press the seam open.

5. To complete the top you will need to sew the two pieces together using a Y-shaped or 'inset' seam as the seam is not a straight line (see fig 3).

To sew the Y-shaped seam, align the edge of fabric 5 to the edge of fabric 1 and sew together. Stop sewing ¼in (5mm) before you reach the centre. Remove the fabric from the machine. Line up the edge of fabric 4 with fabric 3. Carefully sew together from the centre to the edge, starting where you left off.

6. Press all the seams well. If the points at the centre are not matched perfectly don't worry as you will be covering them with a button.

STUFFING THE CUSHION

1. Use the back template to cut a piece from fabric 6, then place the pieced top RS together with this and line up the edges. Sew all around the outside leaving a turning gap on one edge.

2. Trim the seam back to ⅛in (3mm) and turn RS out. Use a turning tool to push right into the corners. Turn the seam inside at the turning gap and press well.

3. Stuff with polyester toy stuffing being sure to distribute it evenly and push it right into the corners. Hand stitch the turning gap closed.

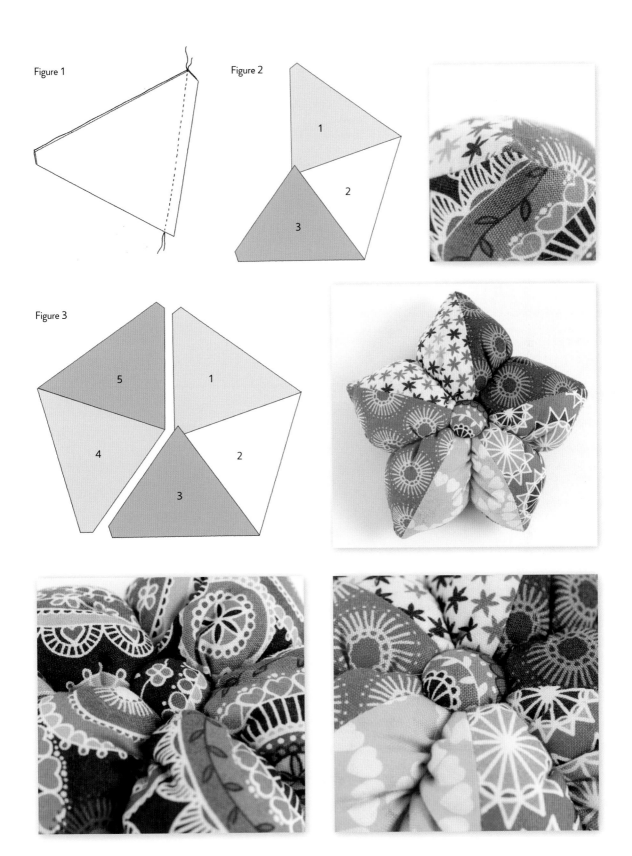

Figure 1

Figure 2

1

2

3

Figure 3

5

1

4

2

3

SHAPE INTO A FLOWER

1. Cover the two self-cover buttons using the 2in (5cm) squares of fabric 6. Do so following the instructions given for the brand of button you have.

2. Thread a strong hand sewing needle with the embroidery thread. Tie a large knot at the end. Push the needle through the very centre of the pieced top and straight through to the other side of the cushion.

3. Line up the thread so it sits directly in the middle of fabric 1. Bring the needle back round to the top of the cushion and feed it through the centre again.

4. Pull the thread tightly so it brings the centre of fabric 1 towards the centre of the cushion forming a v shape. Repeat this so there are now two layers of thread. This should allow you to pull tighter on the thread and deepen the v shape.

5. Continue round the cushion in this way until you have created v shapes in each fabric. This will form the five petal shapes.

6. Using the same thread and without casting off, sew the two buttons to each of the flower centres.

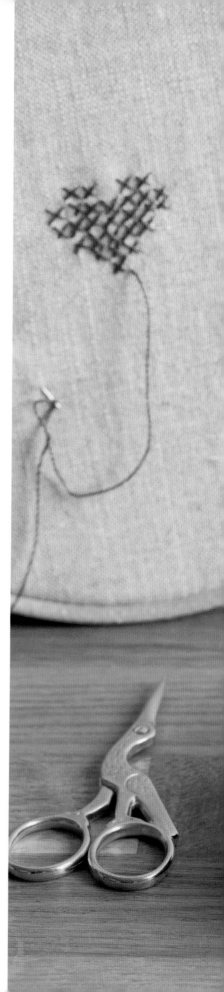

A PERFECTLY PETALLED PLACE TO PUT YOUR PINS

HEXI NEEDLECASE

This simple little needlecase will be in your sewing kit for years to come. Its cleverly pieced hexagons create a perfectly co-ordinating front and back and may just inspire you to make some matching accessories.

Experience level: medium

Techniques needed: rotary cutting, quilting, using templates

YOU WILL NEED

- Fabric 1, one 1½ x 22in (4 x 55cm) strip and one 5½in (14cm) square

- Fabric 2, one 1½ x 22in (4 x 55cm) strip and one 5½in (14cm) square

- Fabric 3, one ¾ x 22in (2 x 55cm) strip

- Cotton wadding (batting), 11 x 5½in (28 x 14cm)

- Felt, 5in (12.5cm) square

- Co-ordinating thread

- Sewing kit (see Materials)

- Two co-ordinating buttons

- Hand sewing needle

- Rotary cutter and ruler

- Turning tool (such as a knitting needle)

NOTES

All seam allowances are ¼in (5mm) unless otherwise stated.

WS = wrong side(s)

RS = right side(s)

A walking foot is recommended for quilting

Templates can be found at the end of this book

PIECING THE HEXAGONS

1. Sew the three strips together with the narrow one (fabric 3) in the centre. Press the seams away from the centre strip. Ensure you press neatly and keep the seams as straight as possible.

2. Lay the strip RS up on a cutting mat. Starting at one end use the rotary cutter and ruler to cut off the end at a 60-degree angle. Most quilting rulers will have a 60-degree line marked on it or you may also use a specific 60-degree ruler (see fig 1).

3. Turn the ruler over and cut at the opposite 60-degree angle to form a triangle (see fig 2).

4. Continue to cut in this way until you have 12 triangles. You will notice that there are two different versions, one with fabric 1 at the point of the triangle and one with it at the base (see fig 3). Separate the triangles into piles of the two types.

5. From the first pile take two of the triangles. Sew them together along the cut edges carefully lining up the centre stripe. Press the seam open (see fig 4). Trim any excess parts of the seam visible on the right side.

6. Sew a third triangle in the same way. Again, press the seam apart and trim excess fabric. You will now have a half hexagon. Repeat for the other three triangles.

7. Sew both halves of the hexagons together ensuring the centre strips are aligned as neatly as possible. Press this seam open and trim the excess fabric.

8. Repeat these steps with the second pile of triangles. You will now have two different hexagons.

Figure 1

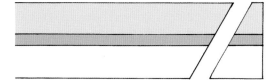

Figure 2

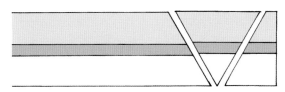

Figure 3

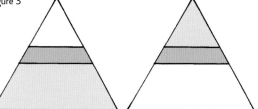

Figure 4

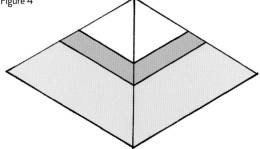

QUILTING THE HEXAGONS

1. Cut the wadding (batting) in half to make two 5½in (14cm) squares. Take one of them and place the first hexagon, RS up, centrally on top. Quilt lines as shown in figure 5

2. Cut away the excess wadding around the edge of the hexagon. Take one of the 5½in (12.5cm) fabric squares and place the quilted hexagon centrally on top RS together.

3. Sew around the edge of the hexagon leaving a turning gap on one side. Trim the seam to ⅛in (3mm) apart from at the turning gap.

4. Turn RS out and finger press to manipulate the hexagon into shape. Use a blunt pointed turning tool like a knitting needle to push into the corners of the hexagons. Carefully turn the seam inside at the turning gap. Pin in place and press well.

5. Sew around the outside ⅛in (3mm) from the edge closing the turning gap in the process. Repeat with the other hexagon.

COMPLETING THE CASE

1. Using the template cut the felt square into a hexagon shape. Sandwich it centrally between the two quilted hexagons with the pieced sides facing out.

2. With the edges of the hexagons lined up, place one of the buttons in the middle of one of the hexagon centres. Holding it in place, put the other button directly on the other side in the other hexagon centre. Hand sew the two hexagons together going through the holes of both buttons as you sew.

....

T I P

Add more than one piece of felt to the inside of the needlecase to store more needles.

....

Figure 5

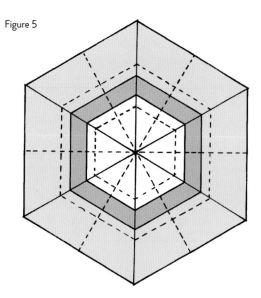

CURVY COASTER SET

Test your paper piecing skills on this charming coaster set – you'll be surprised at how achievable curved seams are. A simple small scale project such as this is perfect for extending yourself by trying a new technique, and at the end of it you'll have the perfect spot to put down that well-earned cup of tea or coffee!

Experience level: advanced

Techniques needed: paper piecing, sewing curved seams, quilting

YOU WILL NEED

For the pieced tops (approximate amounts):

- Fabric 1 (cream/background), 30in (76cm) square
- Fabric 2 (orange), 9in (23cm) square
- Fabric 3 (yellow), 9in (23cm) square
- Fabric 4 (navy blue), 6in (15cm) square
- Fabric 5 (pink), 6in (15cm) square
- Fabric 6 (medium blue), 5in (12.5cm) square
- Fabric 7 (light blue), 5in (12.5cm) square

For the rest of the coasters (exact amounts):

- Cotton wadding (batting), 10in (25cm) square
- Fabric 1 (cream/background), 10in (25cm) square
- Co-ordinating thread
- Sewing kit (see Materials)
- Turning tool (such as a knitting needle)

NOTES

All seam allowances are ¼in (5mm) unless otherwise stated.

WS = wrong side(s)

RS = right side(s)

PIECING THE TOPS

1. This pattern uses the foundation paper piecing method to piece the top. Please see the separate instructions in the Techniques section for how to do this. Each coaster has four paper pieced parts so you will need four copies of each piece to make the set.

2. Take a completed B piece and clip the inside of the curve. Make cuts just under ¼in (5mm) long and approximately ¼in (5mm) apart (see fig 1).

3. Take a completed A piece and carefully pin the clipped B piece to it. Start in the centre of the curve, lining up the centre seams of the two pieces. Then work your way to the edges easing the B piece to the shape of the A piece as you go. The cuts in the B piece will make it easier to shape it into position. It may take a little time to do this. Remember you are shaping the B piece to the curve of the A piece not the other way round.

4. Sew the A and B pieces together removing the pins as you go. Carefully press the seam towards the B piece easing the curve into shape as you do so.

5. Repeat this process to add the C and D pieces. Sew the remaining three coaster tops in the same way.

QUILTING

1. Cut the wadding (batting) square into four equal squares. Take one completed pieced coaster top and place it RS up on top of one of the wadding squares. Quilt it according to figure 2.

2. Cut away the excess wadding around the outside of the square. Then repeat for the remaining three coaster tops.

FINISHING THE COASTER

1. Cut the 20in (50cm) fabric 1 square into four equal squares. Take one and place one of the coaster tops centrally on top, RS together.

2. Sew around the outside of the coaster top leaving a turning gap in one of the sides. Trim the seam back to ⅛in (3mm) on the three sewn sides, and trim to the edge of the coaster top at the turning gap.

3. Turn RS out and finger press the outside. Use a blunt pointed tool such as knitting needle to press into the corners. Turn the seam inside at the turning gap and pin in place. Press well and sew around the outside ⅛in (3mm) from the edge closing the turning gap in the process. Repeat this for the remaining three coasters.

Figure 1

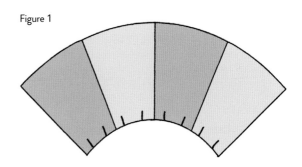

Figure 2

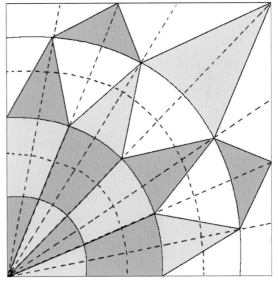

NATTY NOTEBOOK COVER

· ·

The clever element in this book cover design
is the fact that you can use a pen or pencil to
fasten it closed, making it just a bit more likely
that you'll always have one handy when you
need it! Great for jotting down design ideas and
fabric choices.

· ·

Experience level: beginner

Techniques needed: quilting

YOU WILL NEED

- Fabric 1 for the outer cover, 9½ x 17in (24 x 43cm)

- Cotton wadding (batting), 10½ x 18in (27 x 46cm)

- Fabric 2 for the lining, 10½ x 18in (27 x 46cm)

- Fabric 3 for the centre strap, 2½ x 8½in (6.5 x 22cm)

- Fabric 4 for the outer straps and handle, 2½ x 22in (6.5 x 55cm)

  You could use 2½in (6.5cm) pre-cut strip roll/Jelly Roll strips for fabrics 3 and 4 in this project

- Co-ordinating thread

- Sewing kit (see Materials)

- Turning tool (such as a knitting needle)

- Hardback A5 notebook

- Pen or pencil for fastening

NOTES

All seam allowances are ¼in (5mm) unless otherwise stated.

WS = wrong side(s)

RS = right side(s)

A walking foot is recommended for quilting

The measurements given will fit a standard size hardback A5 notebook but do allow for slight variations in design and adjust measurements accordingly.

MAKING THE MAIN COVER

1. Take the outer cover fabric (fabric 1) and place it face up on top of the wadding (batting) in a central position. Pin it in place around the outside and quilt in a diagonal grid pattern keeping the lines 1½in (4cm) apart.

2. Cut around the outer fabric, discarding the excess wadding. Place face down on top of the lining fabric in a central position and sew around the outside leaving a turning gap in one of the short edges. Trim the seam back to ⅛in (3mm) apart from at the turning gap.

3. Use your turning tool to push into the corners. Press well, turning the seam inside at the turning gap. On the opposite side to the turning gap, fold over 2in (5cm) to the lining side and press the fold well. This will create the sleeve to hold the front cover of the notebook. Pin in place.

4. Starting at the top of this fold sew around three sides, ⅛in (3mm) from the edge, closing the turning gap in the process. You will secure the fold in place also (see fig 1).

Figure 1

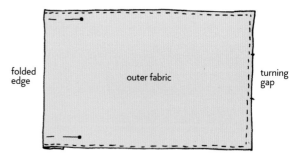

folded edge   outer fabric   turning gap

ADDING THE CENTRAL PEN LOOP

1. Take the fabric 3 strip and fold it in half, RS together, short edge to short edge. Line up the raw edges and sew together down each side. Trim the seams back to ⅛in (3mm) and turn RS out. Use your turning tool to push into the corners and finger press the seams to ensure they are fully turned out. Press well with an iron.

2. Carefully fold the raw edges inside by ¼in (5mm) and line up the folds neatly. Press well. Fold this edge over 1in (2.5m) and press. Stitch in place ⅛in (3mm) from the open edge. Backstitch a few stitches each side to secure. This will create the middle pen loop (see fig 2).

ADDING THE CENTRE STRAP

1. Insert the left cover of the book into the sleeve. Close the book and wrap the rest of the cover around to the front. It will overlap on to the front. Pin the overlap in place.

2. Take the centre strap and place it in the centre of the notebook with the loop ¼in (5mm) from the fold of the overlap. Ensure the back of the loop is facing down and not visible, pin in place (see fig 3).

3. Remove the notebook and the pins holding the overlap. Open the cover out flat. Stitch in place by sewing around the outside ⅛in (3mm) from the edge. Sew directly over the stitch line of the pen loop (see fig 4).

Figure 2

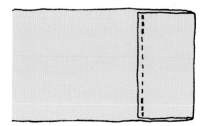

Figure 3

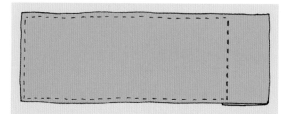

Figure 4

ADDING THE SIDE LOOPS AND HANDLE

1. Once the central loop has been sewn in place, insert the notebook into the sleeve again and pin the overlap back in place.

2. Prepare the fabric 4 as you did for fabric 3 in step 1 of 'Adding the central pen loop'. This time, after pressing the raw edges at the opening, fold over both ends 1½in (4cm) to create the pen loops. Don't stitch down yet.

3. Place the strap so that both pen loops sit either side of the centre one with about ⅛in (3mm) between. Place two more pins in line with the edge of the centre loop. The folded over ends should sit just over the edge of the overlap (see fig 5).

4. Fold the handle round to the back of the notebook. Look at the notebook sideways on from the handle side. Pin the handles in place in the centre (see fig 6).

5. Remove the notebook and open the cover out flat again. Stitch in place with two rectangles starting and stopping where you marked with pins (see fig 7).

6. Place the notebook back inside the cover. Insert a pen or pencil through all three loops to fasten it closed.

Figure 5

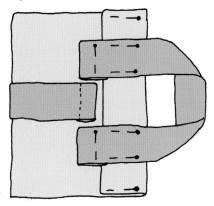

Figure 6

Figure 7

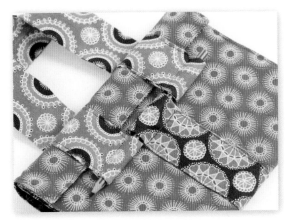

TECHNIQUES

If I have used a technique just once, I have covered how to do it within the relevant project unless it's quite long-winded like paper piecing, but in some cases the techniques are used more often. If that's the case I've provided some how-to guidance here. You can dip back into this section as often as you need.

QUILTING

Most of the projects require a small amount of quilting. A walking foot for your sewing machine is recommended for this. If you don't have one it's still possible to complete the projects using a standard sewing foot.

TURNING GAPS

A turning gap is left if an item is sewn together inside out. The item can be turned right sides out again through the turning gap. When leaving a turning gap backstitch a few stitches either side of the gap to keep it neat when turning.

HAND SEWING

Close turning gaps neatly by hand using a ladder stitch.

USING TEMPLATES

All templates are provided at actual size. They need to be cut out exactly on the line. Draw round a template on the wrong side of the fabric and cut out using sharp fabric scissors.

FINGER PRESSING

This is, as it sounds, squeezing and running your finger tips over a seam to flatten and shape it. It allows you to manipulate a seam accurately into position before you press it with an iron. It is worth taking a little extra time to do this by hand to ensure it is as neat as possible.

FOUNDATION PAPER PIECING

The foundation piecing method uses a paper pattern for piecing. The fabric pieces are sewn directly onto the paper, following the pattern lines, and then the paper is removed afterwards. Each piece in the pattern is sewn in number order. The pieces need to be cut large enough to generously cover all the lines for that piece.

1. Start with the two pieces of fabric that will be '1' and '2' in the pattern. Place them RS (right sides) together with one edge aligned exactly. This edge will be the seam when you sew them together.

2. Hold the pattern with the printed side facing you. Take the two fabric pieces and hold them on the back of the paper, with the WS (wrong side) of fabric 1 facing the paper.

3. Place the seam edge so it overlaps the line between 1 and 2, on the pattern, by ¼in (5mm). It is easiest to do this if you hold the paper up to a light as it allows you to see through the paper to where the fabric edge is and align accordingly (see fig 1).

4. Holding both the pieces in position on the paper sew along the line between 1 and 2. You will be sewing through both pieces of fabric and the paper. Shorten your stitch length to about 30% shorter than you would normally (about four positions on a standard machine). See figure 2.

5. Fold piece 2 over and press into position using an iron. It should extend beyond the lines of its position according to the paper pattern. You should now have both fabric pieces sewn in place, wrong sides to the paper, on the back of the paper pattern (see fig 3).

6. Now fold the paper exactly on the line between 2 and 3. It may help to use a ruler to keep the line straight as you fold. Holding this fold back, on the RS of the paper, trim fabric 2 to ¼in (5mm) from this fold. This will give you the correct seam allowance for sewing the next piece and help you to position it correctly.

7. Unfold the paper and flatten. Take piece 3 and place it in its position RS together with piece 2 (see fig 4).

8. Sew on the line between 2 and 3 (see fig 5).

9. Fold piece 3 back into position and press. Continue in this way until all the pieces in the paper pattern have been sewn. Trim the fabric back to the edge of the paper all round. Carefully remove all the paper.

Figure 1

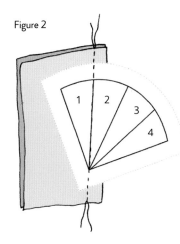

Figure 2

Figure 3

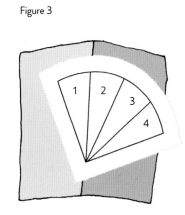

Figure 4

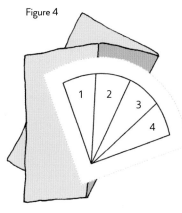

Figure 5

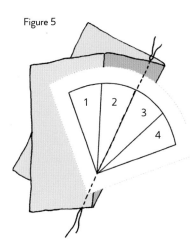

TEMPLATES

Full sized templates can be downloaded
from the Stitch Craft Create website at:
http://ideas.stitchcraftcreate.co.uk/patterns/

The templates printed here are shown at actual size.
Note that only half the Reversible Trinket Bowls
template is provided. Copy it twice and stick the two
halves together along the dotted line to make the
complete the template.

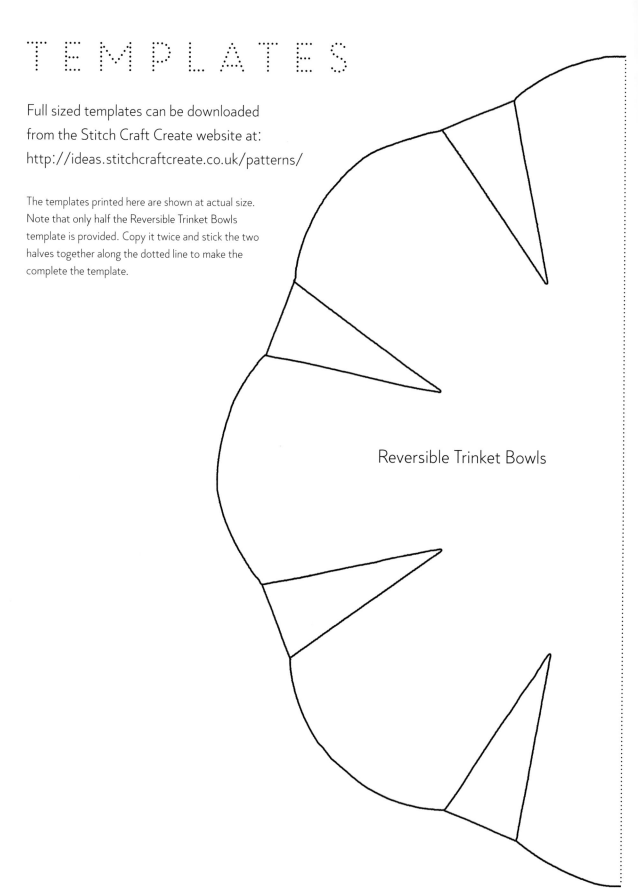

Reversible Trinket Bowls

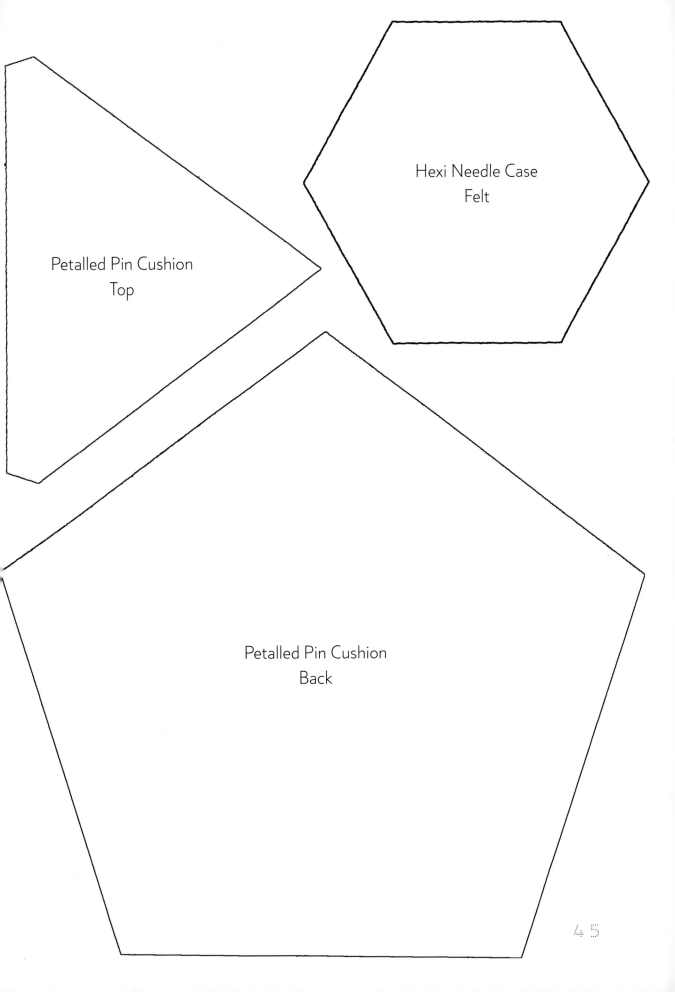

Petalled Pin Cushion
Top

Hexi Needle Case
Felt

Petalled Pin Cushion
Back

45

Curvy Coaster Set

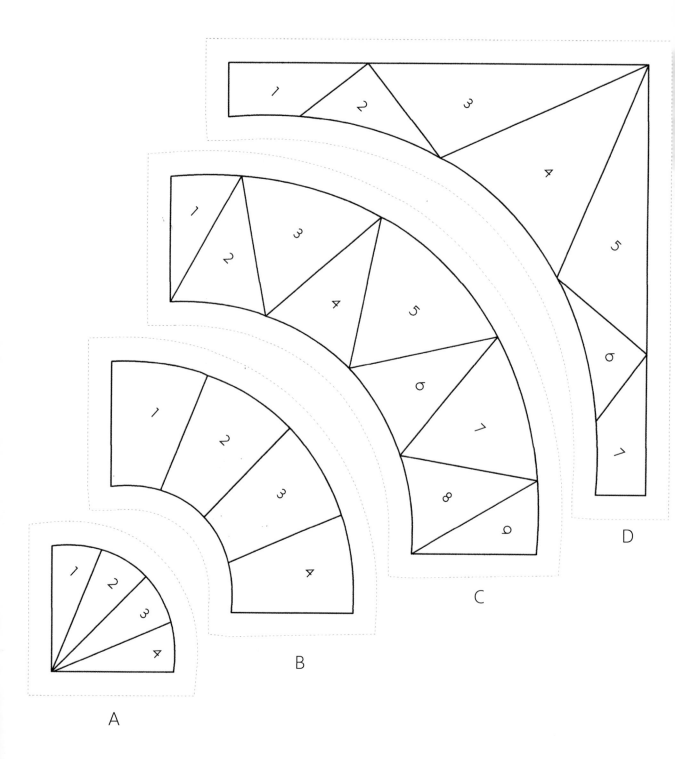

A NOTE FROM THE AUTHOR

Hi, I'm Beth,

I am, and should officially call myself, a 'designer' but I am really just one of those crafty types, who likes making stuff, and always has done. Sewing is my passion. I started making quilts as a teenager and when it got to the 'what to study at Uni?' question there wasn't really anything else I was passionate about. So I studied textile furnishing design in London. This is where I broadened and polished my sewing skills and learned how to 'design' stuff more purposefully.

My creative juices then went on the back burner for a bit in my mid twenties, I was too busy enjoying being young and living in London! It was when I had my son at 28 that I started to get creative again. It was really for the purpose of staying at home with him but being able to work a little too and once I started up again I couldn't stop!

I set up online shops selling bunting, book covers, cushions etc, and then began converting some of my past projects into sewing patterns. I sold many of these to magazines and have now had dozens of my designs published. I still love seeing my projects in print as craft magazines were such a passion of mine as a child.

I came to fabric design by chance after hearing that Makower were looking for fresh blood. I had done a module on print design at University but had no real experience. However, I think as a quilter, and just a lover of fabric, I knew what I wanted to achieve. My first fabric collection Henna hit the shops in October 2013, and I have produced three more collections since.

Alongside the fabric I also have my own pattern business which is going from strength to strength. I sell both digital and printed versions of all my designs and they are available to buy no matter where you are in the world.

Visit my website at www.lovefrombeth.com to find out the latest news.

SUPPLIERS

Love From Beth
For fabric, magnets
and sewing equipment
www.lovefrombeth.com

Stitch Craft Create
For fabric and haberdashery
www.stitchcraftcreate.co.uk

Sew and So
For needlecraft products
www.sewandso.co.uk

© F&W Media International, Ltd 2016

David & Charles is an imprint of F&W Media International, Ltd
Pynes Hill Court, Pynes Hill, Exeter, EX2 5AZ

F&W Media International, Ltd is a subsidiary of F+W Media, Inc
10151 Carver Road, Suite #200, Blue Ash, OH 45242, USA

Text and Designs © Beth Studley 2016

Layout and Photography © F&W Media International, Ltd 2016

First published in the UK and USA in 2016

Beth Studley has asserted her right to be identified as author of this work in accordance with the Copyright, Designs and Patents Act, 1988.

A catalogue record for this book is available from the British Library.

ISBN-13: 978-1-4463-0630-7 paperback
ISBN-10: 1-4463-0630-5 paperback
ISBN-13: 978-1-4463-7457-3 PDF
ISBN-10: 1-4463-7457-2 PDF
ISBN-13: 978-1-4463-7458-0 EPUB
ISBN-10: 1-4463-7458-0 EPUB

10 9 8 7 6 5 4 3 2 1

Acquisitions Editor: Sarah Callard

Desk Editor: Michelle Patten

Project Editor: Jane Trollope

Art Editor: Anna Wade

Photographer: Jason Jenkins

Production Manager: Beverley Richardson

F+W Media publishes high quality books on a wide range of subjects.

For more great book ideas visit: www.stitchcraftcreate.co.uk

Layout of the digital edition of this book may vary depending on reader hardware and display settings.